SELL A BRAND

SELL A BRAND

...Convert your potential energy into kinetic energy

Kwame Boachie (MD), Meninchie

To order additional copies of this book, contact:
Xlibris
844-714-8691
www.Xlibris.com
Orders@Xlibris.com
817015

CONTENTS

Special thanks to Naana for reading over my first
draft and giving me the needed support.

Introduction

If you want to create a lasting impression in the universe, you have to be a brand. All the big-name brands you have heard of today were brought about by a human, like you.

A brand is a name, term, design, symbol, or other feature that distinguishes a person, organization, or product from its rivals in the eyes of the consumer.

Everyone has something to sell to the world. Regardless of how you see yourself, there is a product within you which the world is waiting to get a feel of. It may be singing, boxing, running, coaching, acting, leadership, catering, sculpturing, drawing, etc.

There are several kinds of branding, but the scope of this book will cover personal branding and the need to be a personal brand. At times, personal branding and product branding may be inseparable; your personal brand is a visual representation or embodiment of who you are as an individual. It is your uniqueness. To simplify the terms "personal" and "product brands," I will give an example: Oprah Winfrey is a personal brand while OWN (Oprah Winfrey Network) is a product brand. Your personal branding to a large extent affects the patronage of your product or services since a formidable product stems from a formidable personal brand.

Building your product upon a well-built personal brand is easier and better than doing the converse. Note that product brands and personal brands are not mutually exclusive so don't live with the illusion that whatever you decide to do in your "private life" will have no effect on your products and services. An exception, however, is when you are either able to totally conceal your private events from the public or when you take a back seat in the affairs of your products and services. Hence if your "private" life will not promote your product or services, keep it truly "private."

History shows us so many esteemed product brands, businesses, organizations, and companies that took a nosedive because the prime owners paid less attention to their personal branding. Examples are the numerous celebrities who have fallen far below the pinnacle of their careers because of involvement in scandals, which marred their personal brands. No business would want to be associated with a wife beater, child molester, serial killer, drug addict, chronic alcoholic, etc., no matter how charming you look or how many Grammys, Nobel Prizes, or Oscars you have under your belt.

You could go to school to acquire business diplomas to come up with a great product brand, but if you neglect your person as the chief component of your brand, all your hard work can be likened to building a tower on quicksand. If you want to have a sustainable product brand, you would need to have a "solid" personal brand, which this book seeks to expound.

Everyone on earth is relevant but you only *become a brand* when you are able to sell your *relevance*. It is therefore not enough to claim self-importance when others don't get a feel of you. Humans were made in the image of their Maker. In fact, the Creator wanted to share His nature, that was why humans were created. It is for this reason that humans also have the "creation" ability. You are not made to be selfish. You can't become great when you withhold your potentials.

Likewise, birds cannot fly if they restrict their wings; they are only able to soar to greater heights by spreading their wings. This theory is apparent in the developmental differences between developed and developing communities; how one is more advanced in terms of infrastructure than the other. Developed communities create things with global applicability while most developing ones feel fulfilled and satisfied with inventions of local applicability. There is so much more that can be done! Where one sees an opportunity in every thought and dream, the other limits its ability to its mediocre achievements.

You are unique, and your DNA says it all. You alone can do what you do, exactly! You being a *brand* is your "added value" that allows you to command more in your niche.

Ships don't sink from external forces but by their own internal imbalances, so don't sink yourself!

In this life, everyone has the full complement of what it takes for him or her to be successful. It is an inherent property! You have already survived a tougher competition to get to be on this earth. The millions of spermatozoa that missed the ovum of your biological mother for you to get the chance to get fertilized and come into existence shows that you are already a survivor. Just as it is in human female fetuses who have their full set of ova (eggs) already by the time they are born, you are already equipped with potential. The height of your capability is what is termed "greatness," and you can reach it if you only know and follow the path or, in some cases, carve out the path that leads there. Greatness is within, not without.

This book's focus is not only to help you "discover" who you are; it is also geared toward making you aware that you indeed are! It has been authored through inspiration, deep reflective thinking, amalgamation of life experiences, and thorough research.

This read is meant for those who have given up in life, those in pursuit of success, as well as those who are already up in life's journey toward excellence. It is for entrepreneurs, doctors, lawyers, pilots, presidents, kings, queens, athletes, musicians, comedians, actors, salespersons, sailors, soldiers, and everyone who draws breath and certainly for you, the holder of this book. To anyone who seeks excellence, these pages have been custom-written for you.

The ensuing chapters seek to guide you toward the path of living the greatness that you already are. Take all you can from this great book and run with it.

ONE

Do a good work

Whatever you do, do well. For when you go to the grave, there will be no work or planning to knowledge or wisdom.

Ecclesiastes 9:10, NLT

The above statement was made by King Solomon, the wisest man in history who is believed to have ruled Israel from 970 to 931 BCE.

Everyone appreciates good things. This is not surprising because our Creator, whose image and likeness we were made in, liked good things from the beginning of the world.

"Then God looked over all He had made, and He saw that it was very good" (Gen. 1:31a, NLT). Everything created by the Creator is an original, and whether you believe it or not, you were created to be *unique* and *original*. You are not just a product of calculation, probability, divisions, and duplications of cells or by chance. You are unique and there is only one of you in this world now and even the world to come. You are an original and you are a *good thing*. The reason why we are naturally inclined to like unique things is that a unique thing satisfies a need exclusively. Things that are original and unique may be hard to come by, but they are easy to identify. You remember that moment when you quickly replaced an earlier item you picked at a shop when you finally came across the exact one you had been looking for? That is the feeling of encountering an original! *For the purpose of discussion and to avoid repetition, wherever you come across "yourself" in this chapter, you can assume I am referring to "your brand."*

Remember, you are *the* original and like gold; you can't reinvent yourself, you can only refine yourself. And this can only happen when you are able to "discover" yourself. The competitor of your tomorrow is yesterday, not any person anywhere and definitely not today, because today is the platform for you to work on yourself. The version of you yesterday, which you are not pleased with, can change tomorrow only if you are willing to work on yourself today. All it takes to start is *a will*. You, therefore, have no business brooding today because today is work time! Some say the secret of success is hard work, others say it is smart work; whichever of them it is, there definitely is "work" involved. Working is not a curse. Every human has to work. The first principle of *Sell a Brand* is to *do a good work*. So combining all that has been said so far, one can rightly conclude that the chapter title simply means *be the good work*. This is because you become what you do.

Imagine having a one-man chopper and wanting to travel from one city to another in the shortest possible time. Having the chopper is a good start, but your chopper will only take you to your destination if you become its pilot, not just a passenger. Your desired future can only come to pass when you are able to become the person who lives in that future. Like the world we see around us with its vast technological advancements, these did not come about by chance but because the dominant inhabitants, humans, consciously put in efforts to turn things around. Indeed, it takes a twenty-first-century human to survive in a twenty-first-century world. We are all traveling with one-man choppers in this world. No one will take you to your destination but you. You must be your own pilot!

You were created as a good product, so don't market a bad product as your brand. Be diligent with yourself. Note that gold and crude oil are of no use to anyone in the soil. Their usefulness becomes apparent once they have been refined and processed into jewelry and fuel respectively. Therefore, working on yourself to bring out the "mineral" in you is the first step to take, in order to *sell a brand.*

I read an interesting post on the internet which suggested roads and highways be named after the contractors who build them, including their home addresses and offices instead of after heads of state and historical figures. It sounds cynical, but if such was done, the engineers who build roads that can't stand even one seasonal cycle will sit up and give their best. Good work is rewarded with a good name; material wealth may follow.

Many people today will choose material wealth over a good name any day, but they forget that you can't buy *a good name.* There is an Akan proverb whose literal translation goes "When you install yourself as king, don't expect loyal subjects." The truth is, it is easier making material wealth after having a good name than the converse. In the twenty-first century with its social media, this is even easier. All you may need to be filthy rich is to have a vast number of followers and you can monetize practically anything! So if you want to become wealthy, make making a good name your priority.

Money-making trends change with the ages. For example, in the nineteenth century, the world's wealthiest men were mostly industrialists: Cornelius Vanderbilt, also known as "The Commodore," John Davison Rockefeller, and Edward L. Doheny are few of such people. Then in the twentieth century, trading in commodities such as oil and gold churned out magnates such as Mir Osman Ali Khan, J. Paul Getty, as well as real estate tycoons like Yoshiaki Tsutsumi. The twenty-first-century richest people are mostly linked to technology, for example, Microsoft founder Bill Gates, Amazon founder Jeff Bezos, Facebook founder Mark Zuckerberg, and the list is endless. The trends in becoming wealthy is like the wind; it is very unpredictable where it may blow toward. However, one thing is certain: when you make a good name for yourself, you can sell practically anything to reach the top of the success you seek. "Good names" have opened so many doors than material wealth could only dream of knocking at. Material wealth does not make you a brand; a good name does! You may be the richest person per your judgment, but if you do not have a good name, you are not relevant and you are simply *not a* brand. Popularity has never been equal to a good name, and despite modernization, technology, liberalization, and all, this will not change. Popularity goes away as cheaply as it comes. As a matter of fact, anything you do to get people's attention can gain you popularity. It usually doesn't last unless you attach a good name to it. Using your good name to get people's attention will be discussed later on in chapter 6. Nature does not compromise. It doesn't matter how difficult it is to pronounce your name; when you do a good work on *yourself,* everyone would be forced to learn your name, including its phonetics.

There are no bad babies, so why are there bad adults? The change is in time and knowledge. The difference between any two people is, therefore, time and knowledge. The kind of knowledge you acquire over time is what will set you apart from others. With time being a constant, the variable here becomes knowledge, which comes about as a result of one's exposure. Bear in mind that exposure does not automatically make a person knowledgeable. There has to be a conscious effort to obtain knowledge. What are you exposing yourself to? Are your exposures good or bad ones? Useful ones or inconsequential ones? It would have been great to get exposure to everything so that you can make informed decisions. However, our limited time frame as mortals with only twenty-four hours in a day, fifty-two weeks in a year, and short lifespan permits only so much that we can be exposed to. You must, therefore, be intentional with the knowledge you acquire. What use is a comprehensive knowledge in suturing a surgical wound to an attorney? Not so much. By all means be curious to understand as much as you can about your surroundings, but don't do so at the expense of acquiring useful knowledge. Time and resources spent pursuing nonbeneficial knowledge is time missed in acquiring helpful ones because even though time is infinite, you are finite. The world is not passing away; it is you who is passing through it, to go away from it.

You need to love yourself enough to want to spend on your own betterment. Mind you, this is not equal to selfishness. It is essential for you to make yourself useful enough to better serve others. It is for this reason that even in passenger airplanes, one is asked to fix their own face masks first before attempting to fix that of others in the event of an emergency landing. Placing yourself in a position to offer help is as important as the help you profess to offer. For example, you can't give love if you don't love yourself. If the goal is to serve only one's interests, then that is when selfishness comes in.

You are your greatest asset, so you need to invest in yourself first. There are so many ways one can invest in oneself. It starts from feeding your mind to readying your feet. You surely have to work on *yourself* if you plan on working on anything or anyone. You must have a mental picture or vision of where you aspire to be, always.

You are worthy of all the resources needed to achieve excellence. Everything a person knows, they learned it. Learn!

1. Learn to be a good person

You can't be crappy and expect to sell out a good product. Good morals is a core business attribute that cannot be neglected if you want to be relevant. Your presence on earth is to occupy a position and not just to occupy space. You more than matter because you are not just mass, but you have weight and potential as well. You metamorphose into a force when you actually mobilize your potential and move toward a target!

The fact that you occupy a position makes you a vessel to help others. Develop the attitude of helping people personally, not only remotely. No matter how introverted you are as a person, you have to learn to reach out to others, even if you have to do so in your own way. Develop genuine concern for the well-being of others. It doesn't come easily, but with practice, it will become a habit. Bitterness from past relations and experiences may make you resentful toward people. It may make you lose hope in humanity entirely. It may even be initially difficult for you to connect with people, but you have to acknowledge that until old bridges are pulled down, newer and better ones can't be built in their stead.

You surely are stronger than your emotions, so do not let them control, rule, and ruin you! It may interest you to know that you can gain all the knowledge and market the best product ever, but if your product's core aim is not to help people, it will not stand the test of time.

It is good to make money out of your product, but you need to put your customers' satisfaction above your profit if you wish to make any profit at all. I can't emphasize this point enough, but the purity of the water testifies of its container's lining. Consumers can tell if you are genuinely interested in meeting their needs or you are only interested in making money off them.

Have values and be known for them by living up to them. Having values—"good" ones, of course—does not make life easy for you, but it does make things simple. Your values can serve as your algorithm, which keeps you in check when you are veering off-course. Apart from primitive reflexes, whatever a human does, he/she has thought about it before. Your embodiment is usually your "walking mind." Start with your mind and your mindset. Whatever you spend time thinking about is what often materializes, so think good and your product will come out so.

When your mind thinks of something good to benefit mankind, your hands won't do otherwise. If for some reason you "think" you have good intentions/ideas/plans but you are producing substandard end products or services, evaluate your thinking. One thing that can guide you to have the right thinking is to not get too engrossed with the gains of your product (it is good as motivation though), but consider how the product is going to better the one on the receiving end.

You must also have integrity as an entrepreneur. That is, doing what is right and honest over what is fun, easy, and quick. Integrity should be that value that you hold on to, even if you have to go down while holding on to it. Later on, as your brand grows, the more and more integrity and reputation would matter and the less technical skills would matter. This is because once you have advanced as a brand, your technical skills would be irrefutable. It is said that lions do not eat grass, not because of pride, but it is just not in their nature. People feel safe and certain when they are dealing with people with intact integrity because they are assured of their unwavering stance. Integrity earns you the trust of others.

2. Learn to be open-minded

We live in an ecosystem where each system communicates with one another. We are made to relate with other people as well as with other ideas that may be different from our own. It is not prudent to set out to make enemies, so when you make some accidentally, welcome them! People should feel free to share their ideas with you, no matter how antagonistic it may be to yours. Position your ears like a funnel and your brain like a sieve, to wit, give a listening ear to everyone but sift the helpful ones from the lot.

You would be amazed by the things you can learn from the least expected places and people. By all means, keep company with those who share your passion and goals, and motivate you, but do not neglect to pay attention to the shortfalls of those who towed a path similar to yours. Everyone and everything in life has a lesson or two to teach you. You should make it a point to learn something from everyone who comes across your path each day, as well as every situation you find yourself in, because the lessons of life are taught on a daily basis and its valedictorians are the open-minded. Since you are going to be interacting with other brands, you ought to learn to accept that other people will have ideas that might not resonate with yours but eventually serve the need of the society.

At this point let me make it clear that fanatism in any form does not foster growth. Be tolerant and receptive of other ideas, yet discerning. The root cause of turmoil, violence, and wars in most war-torn nations is fanaticism of one form or the other. Even among people of the same religious sect, there is so much unrest because of intolerance toward one another's belief. Our differences in opinions, race, beliefs, and culture should bring about harmony and promote collaborations, just like the blend of the black-and-white keys of a piano produces beautiful melodies. Our differences should unite us, not divide us. If your beliefs infringe on the liberty and basic rights of others, rethink them. You don't have to agree with everyone, but you need to tolerate everybody.

3. **Learn to expect nothing from anyone**

Disappointment discourages. It is good for others to come through for you, but you shouldn't live your life expecting favors from people because mortals will always be mortals; they have limits. People may fail you consciously or inadvertently, even the ones with the purest of intentions for you. There is however no disappointment for an "unpointed" man. An unpointed person is one who isn't anticipating anything from someone or somewhere. He/she cannot be bothered if help comes or not. Such people are at times referred to as "carefree."

Everyone who wants to achieve greatness must learn to be "carefree" with their expectations. Let expectations be the wind to augment your effort but not the oars to paddle the boat of your brand. This will save you from many heartaches. You have to learn to be both a planner and an executor. It is noteworthy that the greatest CEOs were at one time the janitor, receptionist, security, secretary, treasurer, and PRO of their brands. At times you just have to be able to do it all.

It is good when you have help, but overly relying on it could be a dream killer. It is wise to consider help as a bonus to your effort but not the main driving force. Be prepared in and out of season! Have independent ideas and develop them by yourself when you are starting out any venture. Once you are certain of the path you are towing, you can solicit help or get others on board.

Do not be afraid to start your business alone! The proverbial "eagles fly alone, pigeons flock together" should be your mantra at the developmental stage of your brand. Don't rush your beginning phase. It is not lonely only at the top; it is also lonely at the bottom when you are starting out. Embrace the solitude and develop the spirit of being independent. You need to crawl before you walk and walk before you run. Do not be too quick to seek "support" from others. You do not want to come out as too needy. The next chapter will talk about "standing up for yourself." Before you can stand up for yourself in the midst of the crowd, you should have strong "feet" and these are built during your solitude.

4. **Learn from those who know**

   Every venture you find yourself in, you need to have adequate knowledge concerning it. Knowledge in simple terms means acquisition and assimilation of new information. The new information you need comes to complement you, not to substitute what you already are. This is the balance between *nature and nurture.* Within the nucleotide sequences of your DNA is you as a *brand,* but like every raw material, you need to be processed into a finished product. Nature has ways of bringing out both the best and the beast in you; nurture, however, offers a more controlled and conscious method of processing your raw state. Knowledge acquisition is one of the most important modes of nurturing. "Seeking" knowledge is paramount as knowledge does not diffuse by *passive transport* but by active searching. Even if someone were to offer you information freely, you must be ready to receive it and imbibe it to make it useful. The information you acquire must transform you into a better version of yourself.

   Since your product is meant to meet the need(s) of people, it is important to acquire the knowledge needed for interacting and associating with people as well. When you seek knowledge, seek one which will help you in your field of work. There is so much out there, but not everything is beneficial to you. Enrich your mind because no beauty surpasses a beautiful mind. Aristotle rightly said, "Those who know, do; those that understand, teach." Therefore before you *do,* you must first *know*. Learn from someone who knows and knows *well* because oftentimes a student is as bad as the master. The converse also holds true. You don't have to turn out like your teacher, you have to be better than him/her, but not until you have been duly taught. During the learning process, stick with the adage "No servant is greater than the master." Be teachable because no sane person bakes an already baked cake; to wit, no teacher will be willing to teach you if you come across as a know-it-all. You must employ all your senses of perception in the learning process, no matter your trade. Besides, at this point, this is the only "tool" you have. The plural "tools" was not used because all the senses sum up as one, hence inseparable.

- You must look before you leap.
- You must listen intently; not just wait, so you can speak.
- You must be able to "sniff" opportunity from miles ahead.
- You have to practice to perfect.
- You have to taste success to know how failure will taste like.

In our modern world, there are several teachers such as traditional mentors, celebrities, role models, peers, and social media. The modes of teaching may be different, but what is important is to know who your teacher is. Don't allow just anything or just anyone to feed your mind. Note that, not every person who is successful at their careers is successful at real life. Choose your teachers wisely. I will emphasize that knowledge does not come automatically. In fact, it isn't free or even cheap! Wisdom may be acquired through old age, experience, or nature; knowledge, however, has to be sought after. There is always a price to pay for knowledge: with time, monetary fee, or in kind. See it as an investment when you have to part with one or more of the above-mentioned modes of payment in exchange for knowledge. With the exception of time, you will recoup in thousandfold the rest when you obtain the necessary knowledge and utilize it.

5. **Learn self-control**

Nothing can destroy you from without, without your "permission" from within. The number one killer of *brands* (dreams, aspirations, and success-stories) is lack of self-control at some point during the development of the potential or at the zenith of success. Many great kings and empires have been brought down their knees due to lack of self-control. You are as strong as your weakest point. It is therefore imperative that you identify your weak spots, because you have them. Do not live in denial of your weakness because even the great ship *Titanic,* whose engineer boasted "Even God cannot sink this ship," sank on its first voyage! When you know your weakness and guard it well, it will take extraordinary effort for someone to use it against you. It would be a pity to get to the pinnacle of your brand only to be brought down to your nadir because you could not exercise self-control. A minute of guilty pleasure could ruin years of hard-built reputation.

Do not belittle "anything" that poses a threat against your weakest "spot." Scrutinize everything. It is always better to be safe than sorry. Self-control and discipline do not come easy, but you need to put in the effort to achieve them. You should be able to put a leash on your cravings, feelings, emotions, and whims at all times. Your first subordinate in your journey to success is your body. You should be able to make it subservient to your will and goals. To achieve self-control, you need to be disciplined. If you must wake the body up at dawn to complete a task, do it. If you must starve your fantasy to make an investment, go ahead. If you must hit the gym to obtain the body you desire, do so. Sometimes, you just cannot have your cake and eat it too. Unfortunately, there is no substitute for discipline, but you can get better at it with practice.

It is only when you have done a good work on yourself that you are ready to "create your brand."

TWO

Create a brand

There was a funny meme on social media which read "you are not jollof rice; you cannot please everyone." Jollof rice, by the way, is a special type of rice dish prepared by cooking rice in tomato stew. This dish is a popular West African delicacy that is relished by anyone who tastes it.

It is important to know that you may not be relevant to everyone, but there is definitely someone or a situation in which you are an indispensable tool. Many people look down on themselves because they fail to see their relevance. They even write themselves off in other people's books with no cause. They look for all the reasons why they won't amount to anything even before they start.

No one is more important than you. The fact of the matter is that, until a need arises, nothing is relevant! Trust me, the need will surely arise. You must, however, be in a state of constant readiness or preparedness because opportunity may come knocking unexpectedly. The future indeed belongs to the prepared. Even "luck" materializes when it falls on the lap of ready minds and feet. If you are not prepared, a million "lucks" will pass you by without you even realizing them. And it will be such a pity for the opportunity you had been hoping for to slip away because you were not prepared when it came by.

More often than not, your enemy of progress is the man/woman you see in the mirror each morning when you wake up. Speak to him/her each time and say you can and will do it! Always remember that the only competition you have is with yourself; therefore, you have to know yourself! No one goes to battle without knowing their enemy's weaknesses and strengths. And though it is true that another person can discover your potential, it makes more sense for you to know who you are and what your capabilities are. No one knows you better than yourself because you have been with yourself longer than anyone has been with you. You know your likes and dislikes, what interests you and what irritates you. We are programmed as humans to go after our interests.

The human body releases several hormones, including endorphins, serotonin, and dopamine, which trigger excitement in us when we pursue what we are interested in. It is for this reason that a 70-kilogram man will not break a sweat lifting up his 75-kilogram sweetheart when this same man can't even lift up a 60-kilogram gas cylinder. Interests are usually inherent, and you are more likely to follow through with the pursuit of it than something you do not like. It is only in a few instances that one discovers their interests after trying out several other things. Majority of the time, your interests will be things that you enjoy doing the most, fascinates you, or things you excel at than others. At times too you might not be the best at it, but performing that activity provides you with a sense of inner fulfillment or completeness.

Your interests may not be popular or it might even be too popular; it does not matter. So far as it will fulfill a need in someone else's life, it is worth pursuing. First, say to yourself you can make it happen, and the ability will follow. The question most people ask is, is it possible to achieve everything and anything? The answer is a simple *yes*. This is because there is no impossible goal on earth, just impossible execution plans. Whatever your goal is, with the right plan you should be able to achieve it. This is because even the most complex architecture was once on a drawing table. Put your abilities to good use.

Your abilities should enhance and not destroy though. Remember, you were put here on earth to meet the need of someone. Don't bury your abilities. Your reward is the success that follows in the form of riches, good health, favors, commendations, gratitude, etc. A typical illustration of this is seen in the parable of the master who entrusted his wealth to his servants before leaving for a sojourn. He gave five bags of gold to one, two bags of gold to another, and one bag of gold to the third one, according to each individual's ability. On his return, all but the one who received the one bag of gold had multiplied their share of the wealth. The latter was reprimanded for not utilizing what he received, while those who used their portions were lauded. Even though the master gave them different measures of his wealth, it was expected that each servant put to use their "ability," not necessarily the "gold" given, to earn more. The one with the one bag of gold focused on the "gold" in his hand instead of the "ability" he had.

At the end of the day, our conscience judges us harder on things we could have done but did not do than on the things we did but should not have done. If you withhold your abilities, that might be all you will ever have; no other gains. The servant with the one gold in the parable was resentful of his master for giving him "only" one gold. This is true for most people. You may not have what you see in other people, yet they also do not have what you have. The pinky finger is not less important than the middle finger because it is shorter; each serves a distinctive purpose on the hand to make it whole. It is always easier to blame others when things don't go the way you thought they should. We often forget that when we point a finger at another person, the rest of the fingers point to us. Blaming people, no matter how guilty they are, for your inadequacies will not solve anything. You need to take full responsibility for your own life's journey. You may not get the cheers or push you expect from others in your endeavors. You are not the first; neither will you be the last to experience this. People might not be honest with you; others might even be looking for your disgrace or downfall, but remember, as long as you meet a need, you are still relevant.

Your relevance is your weapon. You may have been put here on earth for only one assignment, and most of the time it is that one thing that makes you restless. Our souls are indeed restless while we live, that is why we bid the dead "rest in peace." So, if you are "resting" while you draw breath, wake up and pursue your purpose. Your purpose may be similar to others, but no two purposes are the same. Someone's assignment was to invent the lightbulb; another's was to develop computers. You have a unique assignment. It may be global or local, but you, as well as the entire world, will never find out unless you unleash it. It comes as no surprise when no one knows you until you have made a great impact! Do not be resentful when such happens. It is not strange because you don't get rewarded for no work done. It is that simple. You are only paid or accorded your worth. Everyone has worth, but until you demonstrate it, no one will take notice of you, and certainly no one will pay you duly.

You do not need a diploma in creative arts to *create a brand*. You already have what it takes: breath of life and unique DNA! Once you identify that *one thing* that makes you unique or that you enjoy doing, the work is half done. You just have to pursue it. I am not suggesting you quit your profession necessarily. It is good to have a profession. It is no secret that most people are in several professions just to get their bills paid. By all means, do what you have to do to survive, but don't forget to "live" while you are at it. You can choose to die rich after having lived a "wasted life" because you lived serving another's *dream* or die fulfilled because you lived your passion. Riches may make you happy but true joy is found in fulfillment.

Research has shown that those who are able to identify and follow their passions tend to be happier and healthier, live less stressed lives, and have a more positive outlook on life. Every channeled passion can pay, and very well too. It depends on how it is utilized! You may just be the trailblazer in that area. The fact that athletes are among the highest-paid professionals currently, which was not the trend a few years ago, shows that your current "nonpopular" passion can also make you wealthy if the right "plugs" are pulled as you pursue it.

Creating a brand essentially means standing up for yourself, taking yourself out of oblivion into existence. You have to believe in yourself first before others can believe in you and buy your product or employ your services. The nostalgia that the name " Ferrari" evokes presently, I believe, was not the same in 1939 when Enzo Ferrari founded his company. People are naturally attracted to confidence. Amid the crowd, you get counted when you stand out! The future indeed belongs to those who believe in the beauty of their dreams. Don't stop dreaming; it is free, anyways! However, do not just dream, live it.

What sets *a brand* apart from just a product or commodity is the bargaining power *a brand* wields. It is not prudent to create just another product on the market because if you do, you will not command a niche market. The importance of niche market cannot be overemphasized. You know your product is *a brand* when people commit solely to get your commodity and none other. Your work should be such that when your commodity is out of stock, consumers will rather return when it is restocked than go home with the alternative. Others may also be selling water as you are, but what may set yours apart may be the flavor you add to it. You may own a restaurant just like others, but what might make your recipe so special for throngs of people to patronize yours may be that extra grain of salt you add or take out. You are unique; don't just blend in with the rest no matter the similarity of your products. You have to be innovative with your product especially when there is already a similar one out there.

When you are *a brand,* your added value allows you to charge more or command more than what identical products command. Brands do not worry about their price tags because their consumers (those who know their worth) are concerned more about having a piece of the product more than they are of the money or possession they are parting with. There may be several professional public speakers out there, but what may make organizations choose you over other notable speakers as a keynote speaker for functions may be your remarkable introductions or sign-offs.

What is within you is worthless until it has been let out. Everyone thinks themselves a great singer until they open their mouth to let out a melody. If Beyoncé had not opened her mouth and had only hummed the tunes of her world-class songs to herself, she would not have known the flaws of pitches that sounded right in her "inner ear," the diction to correct, and the tempos that needed adjusting. When the song is in your mind, sing it out; when you see the picture in your vision, paint it out; when the recipe is in your book, cook it out; when the story is in your memory write it out. Give it a shot because the surest missed shots are the ones not taken! As a pregnant woman carries her baby for forty weeks but meets it for the first time after birth, so is your passion, talent, ambition, and gift. Until you "birth" or bring it into existence, the beauty of your potential will only be a memory.

Brands are *created* and go through processes before they are finally *made.* You must *create* it first, bring it into existence.

At this point, you are your first consumer. Dealing with yourself is tougher than people dealing with you because you could be too hard on yourself or too lenient. One thing, however, that should never be absent is confidence in yourself. Let me reiterate that, people are attracted to confidence. I will sound a caution here to not confuse confidence with arrogance. They may seem similar, but they are very different. The feeling of each as well as their effects differ significantly. Arrogance is destructive but confidence uplifts.

The mathematical distinction between the two is:

Ego+ IGNORANCE= Arrogance

Ego+ INSIGHT = Confidence

Never look down on yourself. Take a cue from the popular adage, "Only look down to admire your shoes." Do not have a bloated ego, but certainly do not belittle yourself or make little your struggles and successes. Also do not be afraid of failures. The revered Thomas Edison was believed to have had 9,999 failed attempts. The 10,000th try was the invention of the light bulb. When asked about all his attempts, Edison replied, "I have not failed 9,999 times, I have simply found 9,999 ways how not to create a lightbulb." Hence it is important to know that failure is the "surest" way to learn while success pampers you to repeat your successes. A "successful" failure incites hunger for excellence.

Do not be hurt when you seem irrelevant in your current circumstance. That does not mean you are a failure. It could be one of the following or both (in rare situations): wrong timing or wrong location. Your relevance as an original is surely needed in this world. The question is when or where are you relevant?

When you are the best version of yourself, you transcend time and place. People will relocate from far and near just to be in your locality when it is the time of your relevance. Your competition too would have no other option than to relocate away from you when you find yourself at the right location of your relevance simply because two captains cannot man a ship. Albert Einstein could have decided to pursue any other venture, but he followed his passion for math and physics and now discussions under these two subjects are not complete without a mention of his name.

Moving on to the fundamentals of creating *a brand,* what do you have to sell? Every great person started from somewhere, and they definitely started with "something." If you are having a hard time figuring out what to brand, there are some few questions that can help you decide on what to pursue:

- What do you want to be remembered for?
- What do you want to be associated with?
- What can't you wait to wake up to? or what are you very passionate about?
- What would you do gladly do, even if you had to do it for free?
- What thing are you the go-to person for?
- What gives you a sense of purpose?

Whatever the above questions brought to bear is what is worth pursuing. When you are convinced within you that something is worth pursuing, often, it is the way to go. Do not look at your surroundings or the crowd to determine if it is the right thing to do or the right time to act. Go with your conviction. If you agree with yourself, chances are the universe agrees with you too! People's opposition to your resolution is not a sign of a wrong move. Take it as a stepping stone because paths with no obstacles often lead nowhere. If what your passion leads you to pursue has been done before, then you have less work to do. This is because those before you would have made most of the mistakes for you to learn from. If you are a pioneer in the field, then you have a chance to pave the way for others. Either way, you have to put in the work to create your brand. Giving up on your passion is not an option on the table of success.

After you have identified what you are passionate about and what you wish to stand for, your brand is created. It may be boxing, piloting, mentoring, baking, sewing, farming, designing, sculpturing, etc.

As a brand, you must have core values and you must stand up for them. There are several of them: honesty, pragmatism, integrity, dependability, reliability, ingenuity, diplomatic, loyalty, efficiency, prestige, positivity, respect, courage, patriotism, perseverance, innovation, service to others, environmentalism, education, creativity. This list is, however, not exhaustive. Although different brands have their unique core values, some of the ones stated above are moral values, which every brand should have. As much as you may want to have all the core values as a brand, it is important that you select only a few of them and be known for them. Choose a maximum of four core values. The fewer your core values, the more satisfaction you are able to offer your patrons since fulfillment will be easier as compared to having numerous core values.

When it comes to being a brand, it is better to be a specialist than a generalist. A specialist is a person who is highly skilled in a specific field as compared to a generalist with capability in several different fields. You command more as a specialist. Remember, you are supposed to be the go-to person. As a specialist, you know more and more about less and less. This makes you more focused and gives you an advantage over a generalist. When you have a cardiovascular problem, you do not go to a general practitioner when there is a cardiologist.

Specialization makes you a guru in your field and brings with it more satisfaction. You may not be the first point of call for people's needs, but when the same people are at their wits' end in your area of specialization, the buck stops with you. You may assume that since the generalist may be the first point of call for consumer needs, they will end up with a large consumer base and the specialist will end up with the "leftovers." This, however, is not entirely so. Between two people who are being showered with money, the one who gathers after the money settles on the ground will collect more with the hands compared to the one who tries to catch them with the hands in midair. This is the illustrative difference between a specialist and a generalist. Specialists get paid more!

I remember during my clinical clerkship in medical school some years ago, we used to welcome patients in the consulting rooms and clerk them (take their medical history) extensively before our attending will come to see them. It served as a learning opportunity for us and also an auxiliary purpose of revealing certain aspects of the patients' clinical histories, which the clinicians often missed with the limited consulting time. Despite the rapport we established with these patients as their first point of contact prior to meeting the attending physicians, when they got well, their gratitude in the form of token and fruit baskets went to the clinicians, not to us the medical students. This is because the relief from their infirmities they sought as they came to the hospital was met via the prescription medications, procedures, and sometimes surgeries our senior colleagues offered them. This is not to say our clerking was inconsequential to the care they received ultimately, but naturally, human gratitude often goes to the one who is deemed to have offered the final and greatest help. Specialize as much as you can.

When you hear of Mercedes Benz, you think of prestige, safety, and exhilarating performance. When people hear of your brand, what do you want them to associate you with?

Brands are known by names, seals, insignia, logo, etc. Sometimes the name you give your brand may reflect what you stand for, but there is no hard and fast rule as to the appropriate name to give your brand. It could be derived from your name or any other source per your discretion. Your brand's name, however, is not as important as the core values you profess to stand for. It is not the image of a bitten apple that intrigues people so much as to put the Apple logo sticker on their properties. It is rather the innovative experience, which patrons derive from the use of Apple products that makes them do so because people like to be associated with great products. If you already have a name for your brand, fair enough, but if you do not have one, do not worry. You can always come up with options and have people help you choose from among them. The essential thing is to focus on developing your core values. Stand up for your interests and be known for your values, and your brand is already created.

THREE

THE BAIT: GIVE OUT A (FREE) SAMPLE

The Oxford Dictionary defines sample as "a small portion or quantity intended to show what the whole is like."

The universal rule "If you wish to receive, you must learn to give" is a very important tool in *selling a brand*. A piece of *you* has to go out before the *whole of you* is "outdoored." This is important for several reasons, and this chapter will do justice to them. The questions that come to mind when giving out a sample are:

- Why should I give out?
- What should I give out?
- Who should I give to?
- When should I give out?

A prudent entrepreneur knows the power in "samples"; they are like baits. They "trap" consumers unknowingly. You really do not lose anything when you give out a sample, but you have all to gain! This might sound like a paradox, but it does not get any truer than that. Bear in mind, "samples" are typically not sold. Whichever niche you find yourself in, give out a free sample. If you are an upcoming musician, organize free concerts. If you are a boxer, collaborate with other boxers and organize free shows. If you are a shirt designer, offer for people to bring their plain shirts to you to design them for free. Lawyers spend so much time and money in school so they do not do pro bono because they are crazy, but because it pays eventually. So the efforts you put into distributing your samples will also pay off in the long run.

Giving out your sample is a means to know how the public will take your brand when you finally *sell* it out because at this point, you are not *selling out your brand* yet. Your resources should be channeled toward producing a quality sample, not an inferior sample with "worldwide publicity."

The sample you give out should not be an inferior version of your brand. Giving anything but an equivalent version of your brand is like showing someone else's image as yours to an online friend. Imagine the disappointment or surprise should he or she meet you in person. You don't want this happening to your brand.

Don't rush through your sample. Be diligent and don't make light of the matter, saying, "But it is 'just' a sample." Many budding entrepreneurs failed because they took their samples for granted. People tend to value things you attach value to. For example, if you start putting trash into your mailbox, very soon passersby will convert it into a trash bin, even when "Mailbox" is clearly inscribed on it. When you value something, you put in your maximum effort; your words alone are not enough! Work and work, until **the** *work is done*. If your brand is the best and you present a slipshod work as a sample, trust me, you have killed your brand before it even started. Someone will then ask, "What about presenting something superior to your brand, as sample?" The reason I did not talk of "not presenting a superior version of your brand" as a sample at the beginning of this paragraph is that it will be tautology. What do I mean? Your brand up to this point is already superior because if you have done a good work as chapter 1 sought to instill, there is only one other way you can go: downgrading. And you do not want to do that. See your sample as a "miniature" of your brand; don't turn it into a travesty. The embryos of most vertebrates, including humans, look the same, but their genetics are different. The human embryo will be born a human being and that carried by a horse will be born a horse. The "genetics" of your sample should be the same as your intended product. As a matter of fact, sometimes your sample may end up being your final product. A sample of Versace cologne is different from the sold version in terms of the size of the bottle, not its content! Do not compromise on the quality of materials you use for your sample.

You do not need a diploma in epidemiology to determine the population of your sample. You could start with your nearest environment: family and friends. Do not be scared of the feedback you may get from them. The next chapter will expound more on "feedbacks." Remember, you are the best there is, so there is no need to fear. If you are a pioneer of your product, it might take some time for people to warm up to your concept/ product, so give it time.

Every good thing takes time. I bet even the family members of the Wright brothers were skeptical to fly their first powered, heavier-than-air aircraft. It is in human nature to be wary of exposure to something one is not used to. You most likely discovered your brand in private, so don't be too surprised or hurt when even your family and friends hesitate to try your (free) sample. Still, give it out. Family and friends give the quickest (not necessarily the most accurate) feedbacks.

Besides family and friends, give your sample out to anyone and everyone else. Give to those interested, those who are indifferent, and even to those who do not seem interested. This will give you a very broad perception of the reception of your sample. Your brand is meant for the universe! Give your sample to someone, and tell them to tell a friend, to tell a friend. We live in a global and technological era so utilize social media platforms to your advantage in distributing your sample. If you are a stand-up comedian, tell your jokes to your family and friends. Post your videos on YouTube, Instagram, Facebook, Twitter, etc. There are countless rich, successful musicians, comedians, models, and actors who started off from social media, especially YouTube, where you could just record videos and post. Examples include Justin Bieber, Carly Rae Jepsen, Soulja Boy, Kate Upton, etc. With YouTube, you could even set up your own station, run it individually, and get paid! As in, you could be your own CEO just by being home and doing videos.

The previously Six Degree of Separation Theory has shrunk to Four Degree of Separation! The degree of separation is the idea that all people are a certain number, or fewer, social connections away from each other.

"The well-known Six Degree of Separation Theory is a rule for the interconnected, globalized age we live in. It states that everyone is connected to each other through others they know by, at most, six rounds of introductions. Because of Facebook, the world is getting even smaller than we have realized. Researchers studying connectedness on social networks have now proposed that 'the average number of acquaintances separating any two people no matter who they are . . . is not six but 3.9!'"- Jessica Leber, 10.28.13 (Fast Company's Co. Exist).

For professionals who interact more with people such as medical doctors, nurses, teachers, flight attendants, etc., this 3.9 could even be less. So the next time you meet someone you don't know, it is an opportunity for your sample to go global. This is because you are essentially only four people away from anyone in the world. This does not mean you have to spend a fortune to send your sample everywhere. Remember that you are giving it out for free. You are not aiming at making "any monetary" gains from it per se, so don't spend too much resources on "marketing."

Be honest to people about it being a sample. Honest brands earn consumer confidence and trust. Studies have shown that even in healthcare systems, practitioners who are sincere with their patients about adverse events resulting in injury to the patients are less likely to be sued than those who are not. The aim of being sincere with your sample is not to gain sympathy per se from your audience, but it shows your authenticity and transparency, which are two important attributes consumers desire from brands. Do not worry about what people may say behind your back about your samples. Do not be afraid of rejection because sometimes it serves as a redirection to better paths. To them, it may be Your Day 1 of your brand. Don't be too hard on yourself because every great master was once a student. When your final product is out eventually after fine-tuning, the pitfalls your sample had will be forgotten.

There are so many successful people who came into the limelight via "unpopular and unconventional" means, but they learned and improved. Now, they are better known by the impact they are making than what they started with. There is indeed no Day 7 without a Day 1. The human mind and heart are attracted to and appreciate free things. Trap these two with a *great* "free" thing and you have won yourself servants for life. To wit, give someone something great they can find nowhere else and they will keep coming back for more. This principle has been employed by successful people throughout history.

It will surprise you to know that people could actually pay to get "free" items!

A case in perspective: In the early 2000s when CDs were very popular, musicians usually went to radio stations to announce the launch of their music albums. During such times, people would call in to talk to the musicians and free CDs were given out to, say, the first three or so callers. The excitement of getting "the newly released album" for free was enough to make these "lucky" winners forget that it actually cost them the same amount of money or even more than the cost of purchasing the album, chartering a cab to go to the radio stations, and redeeming their prizes.

Let me give an unusual example. Those who peddle cocaine give their "targets" free samples to try out, knowing very well the euphoria the substance generates. Once their vulnerable customers get hooked on to it, they then quote hefty prices, and guess what, their customers go to any length to acquire them.

"So, what if my sample does not give people euphoria?" I want to go back and say that every "original" has the ability to cause "euphoria" unless it is adulterated. If you have followed the initial steps of this book and your "sample" is not giving people "euphoria," do not worry. It is a sample for a reason. There may be multifactorial reasons. Your sample is like "the miniature man," human embryo; it has the "genetics" of a man but needs to be born, crawl, and walk, before it can run as men do. Bear in mind that at this stage, you haven't sold your product out yet, so all is not lost. The next chapters will provide guidelines to put your brand on track.

Is there a right or wrong time to give out a free sample? No. Is there a right or wrong method or approach in doing so? Yes. You can turn a wrong timing into a right one if you use the right method. Conversely, you can convert even a perfect timing into a wrong one by employing a wrong method. To explain this, I will give you two scenarios, with the same preamble.

Preamble: Imagine being a cupcake baker and wanting a very busy CEO of a multimillion-dollar company to give your cupcakes to the employees as lunch snack.

The CEO is late for an early-morning meeting and you meet him/her in the elevator lobby.

Scenario 1: You approach him/her and *introduce yourself in the lobby.* The following ensues.

You: Hello, sir/madam. Good morning. Here in my hands are samples of cupcakes I made. My friends and everyone else who has tasted these say they have not tasted anything this delicious. I have read your advertisement for a cupcake vendor to cater to your employees during lunch. Take a bite and let me know what you think.

CEO: [Interrupts you even before your "good morning" could end] I am sorry, young man/young lady. I am late for my meeting. I can't talk now. Some other time.

He/she leaves you at the door and enters the elevator.

Scenario 2: You wait at the door of the elevator with him/her and enter together. You drop one of the cupcakes just at the tip of his/her shoe. The following ensues.

You: I am sincerely sorry, sir/madam (while offering to clean the shoe with a tissue). It is quite unfortunate your shoe got to taste what your lips should have tasted. This cupcake is the best in the entire city and everyone attests to it.

CEO: Really? Who makes them?

At this point, the CEO becomes curious and you have his/her attention! Incite people's curiosity if you wish to convert them into patrons.

There is never a wrong time, only a wrong method/approach.

Sometimes all you might have is just a few seconds to give out your sample. In fact, you do not need to be wordy to convince someone.

In today's busy world, you need to be able to get your sample across to people concisely. Circumstantial speeches easily bore people, especially busy people. When you meet your audience or consumers at a leisure park, you could spend all day to introduce your sample, but when you do not have the luxury of time, the elevator pitch comes handy. It is said that the elevator to success is out of order, so to get to the top, you will have to use the stairs—one step at a time (paraphrased from Joe Girard). True as this statement is, sometimes in life though, a "timely" elevator shows up just about the moment you are about to take the stairs. Should you ignore it? Be discerning.

The elevator ride is not any easier than the stairway and this is why: Consider a young person looking for a job at an esteemed firm and his success at landing this job is to complete the task of getting to the top of a twenty-story building by stairs in twenty minutes or to convince a nonchalant CEO of the firm why he is the right hire within twenty seconds of an elevator ride with him. At the end of either journey, this young person will arrive at the top floor drenched in sweat from physical exertion on one hand or through adrenaline rush on the other. The elevator pitch method is time-bound while the stairway method is tenacity dependent. You can employ these methods in all spheres of life no matter what your brand is about. Sometimes you will have the opportunity to choose which of these two methods to use but it is better to be prepared for both.

As said earlier, the elevator pitch method becomes indispensable to give out your sample when you are time-bound. On an average, an elevator ride takes about twenty to thirty seconds, hence the name. You need to leave an imprint in the minds of your audience with your sample. People's attention and focus are drawn to things they find interesting, memorable, and succinct. Your sample should be able to create all these effects. This means you have to practice to perfect if your sample is an art or an act. Getting family and friends to try out your sample might not require rehearsals, but you do need to be well prepared to be able to get it across rightly when you are introducing it to other people.

The delivery method is as important as the sample itself. There are several different approaches to the elevator pitch method, but the underlying principles are still the same: brevity and persuasiveness. No matter your temperament as a person, you can use this tool. You may be a sanguine with so much charisma or a melancholic who keeps to themselves, but all you need to do is to keep practicing the components and technique for it to be second nature, because such "elevators" usually don't announce their coming!

The basic components are:

1. Introduction: Boldly reveal yourself and your product, highlighting your relevant qualifications.
2. Summary of what your sample (brand) is about: Focus on the problems that your sample/brand solves and how it helps people. You are only relevant to people when you solve a problem in their lives. If you have statistics to back it, briefly state them; if not, do not worry.
3. Your Unique Selling Proposition (USP): Communicate the edge you have over similar brands or your exclusivity. People typically enjoy the feeling of being part of the few to be in on something new or unique.
4. Be ready for questions: Curious minds ask questions, so after indulging your audience with your uniqueness, they most

likely might have a question or two for you so be prepared to answer them. Even if they do not ask you questions directly, always endeavor to leave questions in the minds of your audience to which the answer will be the acquisition of your sample/brand.

Of the four components discussed above, the first one that most consumers/audience are likely to forget after your thirty-second encounter is the first one (the introduction). If the encounter goes very well, you are more likely going to be called back or asked to repeat your introduction, that is, your name.

Research shows that of communication, 7 percent is verbal and 93 percent is nonverbal. This makes the vehicle of delivery of the above components especially vital. To some people, communication may come naturally or easily, but others need to consciously learn and practice the technique of delivery repeatedly.

The technique:

1. Confidence: Express yourself as someone who owns your sample, not as someone who has been handed it to deliver. Remember, you are the CEO and you know more about "it" than anyone else! Do not be afraid. Be bold and courageous. This does not mean be rude or arrogant. Your voice tone forms about 41 percent of your nonverbal communication (38 percent of overall communication), so watch the pitch, rate, and volume. Moderation is key.

2. Body language: Your body plays a major role in communication; it forms the majority (59 percent), of your nonverbal communication (55 percent of overall

communication). Be formal with your gestures and posture. Show enthusiasm but comport yourself, make eye contact, and avoid fidgeting.

3. Believability: You must sound convincing. The sure way others will believe you is for you to believe in whatever you are presenting to them. Keep your words as short and simple as possible. Try to use easily comprehensible words. It is not a literature competition to exhibit your mastery over vocabulary.

You do not need to wait for the "planets to align" before you give out your sample. Any time is perfect time. It will surprise you to know that what you thought was the wrong timing could actually be ideal. Given that it is a sample, it is wise to try it out at different times, so that you can get a cross-sectional idea of its temporality. Quit making excuses with "time." Desist from phrases such as "if only I had time," "if only it were summer," etc. If you have already *created a brand,* then the time to give out your sample is now! Choose your approach well though. We all have twenty-four hours a day; how come some are wealthier than others? The secret is in lack of the right approach, not lack of time.

FOUR

Take feedbacks

> *If you think you are leading, but no one is following, then you are only taking a walk.*
>
> *John C. Maxwell*

Feedbacks are very important. It is the tool you use to evaluate how people took the sample you gave out. There is no successful firm, institution, organization, or enterprise that does not take feedbacks. They may call it different names such as reviews, follow-ups, evaluations, assessment, appraisal, etc. The purpose is still the same: to know whether one is on-course or off-course. There is an Akan adage that states, "He who carves out a path is oblivious of the crookedness he leaves in his wake." If you give out your sample in honesty, chances are you will get an honest feedback also.

Others may help you to give out your samples, but when it comes to taking feedbacks, you must do so personally! It gives you the opportunity to get firsthand information about what patrons liked or disliked about your sample and how you could improve upon it. It is not a time to argue with people about why they did not like your sample. Say "Thank you, I will improve on it" when they express negative views. Never be belligerent over consumer comments or reviews. Be accommodating when receiving feedbacks from people and let them know you appreciate their inputs. Accommodating people's opinions does not necessarily mean you have automatically accepted what they had to say. Position your ears like a funnel and your heart like a sieve when taking feedbacks. Take everything, but don't consume just anything. You must be tactful. Some feedbacks can be discouraging but that should not break your morale. Take note that, the purpose of feedbacks is not for you to "rebrand" yourself or shift course off your target. It is for fine-tuning, so seek frank feedbacks. Dishonest feedbacks are like blunt knives; they give several rugged marks but no true cut. The opposite is the case for frank feedbacks; it directs you appropriately to know what to adjust.

Your brand is for the universe, so take universal feedbacks. Try as much as possible to get feedbacks from all the samples you gave out. Your family and friends are more likely to give you the quickest feedbacks as stated in the previous chapter. They are also the easiest to contact. Ask them to be honest and open with you. Surround yourself with people with positive energy at all times. This is not the time to worry about your feelings being hurt. It is better that your feelings be hurt to your face, so you get to mend your pitfalls, than for your product to suffer rejection behind your back after putting in all the effort and resources. Take constructive criticisms and don't see those who offer them as your enemies.

One positive outlook in life as a budding *brand* is to shun perceiving people, situations, and circumstances that may appear as oppositions, as hindrances. Others may call them enemies or obstacles but see them as stepping blocks and you will be surprised at how far it could unleash your inner strengths and prowess, which you weren't even aware existed. Some people will tell you all the things that are wrong with your brand and give you all the reasons why it will fail. Others may even give you problems to every solution you offer. Don't worry. Sometimes, you hear these kinds of comments more often that you begin to wonder why you even decided to venture into anything. Yes, it could be that discouraging. Be thankful for them anyway. You cannot stop a bird from flying over your head, but you certainly can stop it from building its nest on your head. You can't control what people would feel or might even say about your sample. Some will disguise spite as honesty; others will dress dishonesty as politeness.

It is solely up to you to manage people's reviews. Like former President Franklin D. Roosevelt said, "A smooth sea never made a skilled sailor." So if everyone likes what you are doing, step back and reevaluate yourself. Because even with the tongue, there are different taste buds on it: sweet, sour, salty, bitter. Each of them is essential in appreciating different flavors. It is highly unlikely for your sample to taste "sweet" to everyone, so brace yourself for "bitter" reviews too.

Dealing with feedback is very pivotal in directing the final product of your brand. When analyzing feedbacks, take into consideration the demographics and psychographics of your consumers. People with different characteristics have different tastes. Until you understand your consumers' characteristics, you will not understand their feedbacks and the reasons behind them. This may make you worry unnecessarily based on your misinterpretation of their feedbacks.

Demographics refers to the structure of a given population. This entails the sex/gender, race, age, location, level of education, occupation, profession, and economic status of the sample population. If you take feedbacks in isolation with no consideration of the above, you will end up barking up the wrong tree. Save yourself the needless worry by understanding your sample population. Remember, you gave out your sample to everyone, regardless of your knowledge of their background. When you give your sample via social media, for instance, you expose it to everyone who can access the internet. Although there are audience restrictions on media such as Twitter, YouTube, Snapchat, Instagram, Facebook, Tiktok, etc., due to chain sharing of information, your sample might even reach people you did not intend receiving them. Therefore, you need to be intentional about the things you post on social media. Only post items that you would not mind if they went viral. Within seconds, people at the other end of the world will be able to access your sample when you post it. When you were giving out your samples, the demographics of consumers did not really matter then, but when taking feedbacks, be mindful of that. The reason for giving your sample out to "everyone and anyone" has already been talked about in the previous chapter.

To reiterate it, let us look at an example of why giving your sample to "everyone and anyone" is important. I was once approached by a middle-aged woman who was part of a team offering free screening for hypertension. I was in a hurry and wanted to give her excuses to avoid the screening. She convinced me with just two sentences: "I know you are young and this screening might not be beneficial to you, but the sponsors of this program will not continue to sponsor this project if we do not get at least thirty people coming through at the end of the day. For the sake of those who might benefit from this in future, please pass through and just sign for attendance." I might not have been an "ideal" sample for her, but my participation increased her chances of getting the "ideal" future samples. It is worth noting that there are young people with hypertension though. If I had happened to have hypertension after going in, she would have killed two birds with one stone: gotten a hypertensive enrolled and also gotten sponsorship for future programs. After convincing me, she gave me a souvenir, which consisted of lip balm and nail polish. That was all they had, regardless of the sex/gender of those who got screened. This is also an example of giving out your sample to "anyone and everyone." Although these items were not useful to me, my mother was grateful when I gave them to her after I returned home because she had use for them. You never know where your free sample will end up, especially when you utilize social media. In this twenty-first century, social media can make and break you depending on how you utilize it.

The key uses of social media are networking, business, and entertainment. Unless you have achieved all the success you want to achieve, it would not be prudent to spend all your time on social media entertaining yourself. Sometimes you could even end up feeling depressed when you spend most of your time viewing the glam in people's lives when yours doesn't seem to be all that glamorous. Nobody looks the way they look on social media all day, every day, so don't see yourself as a failure because of something you saw on social media.

Desist from using social media as a "confirmation tool" of whether or not you are a failure in life because its specificity is less than 30 percent; there are too many false-positive lifestyles out there. Utilize its networking and business potentials to your advantage. You could stay in your bed in your pajamas or nightgown and become rich with just a phone, laptop, and internet. With the same tools above, you could also go bankrupt, get depressed, disgraced, robbed, or even get killed. Yes, social media is a double-edged sword; it could be extremely useful and extremely dangerous too. The comment sections of your posts and your inbox are some of the sources of getting feedbacks from your samples. Even though some of your audience may abuse these feedback avenues, you could derive constructive reviews from there too.

That said, taking feedbacks will require you to know and understand the demographics of your sample population. As stated in my aforementioned encounter, I did not have need for the lip balm and nail polish, but my mum did. If the person who gave them to me was looking for feedback, she wouldn't have gotten a good one from me. My mum would have been the best person to give her feedback. If you are a politician and you build a prototype bus terminal for your community and want to find out how it has benefited the people, you don't go about asking those who drive their own cars. You take feedback from those who take public transport.

One of the major reasons why some politicians do not get reelected is because after the polls, they forget to go back to the grassroots, where majority of their votes came from, to take feedback. The same people who made you can unmake you! The true representation of the state of your constituents will not be communicated to you by those you meet at the golf course, VVIP section of the stadia or at the first-class lounge of the airport but by the ordinary man on foot in the park, by the roadside, in the bus, at PTA meetings, in the market.

As stated before, you want to gain feedback from relevant channels or demographic groups that offer a more representative reflection of the entire population because those are more applicable and useful in improving your brand. When it comes to social media, you cannot control who gives you feedback. Using demographics, you should be able to discern which feedback is useful and which one is not. For example, if you are a chef in Ghana who prepares local dishes and you get a distasteful comment on your fufu dish (pounded cassava/plantain) menu you posted on your Instagram page from, say, a non- African living outside Africa (who most likely has never tasted any Ghanaian or African food before), you could disregard such a comment unless his/her comment is about just the appearance of the food. Knowledge of this individual's geographical location and race gives you a hint that he most likely knows next to nothing about the subject of your post. Sometimes people comment below posts for the sole purpose of gaining the attention of the owner of the page. Even though comment sections serve as an important source of feedback, you are not obliged to respond to every comment under your post. For comments that you feel responding to will be inconsequential, you may acknowledge the commentator by selecting the "like" button beside their post instead of typing out a response. If you are already a celebrity, you can choose to interact with your fans, but be careful with your words because there are several predators out there waiting to twist your words. There are different calibers of people on social media, so be mindful. Social media is a jungle. Even though creators and administrators try hard to regulate their platforms, your security and navigation is entirely in your own hands.

In addition to demographics, you want to consider the psychographics or psychological attributes of your sample population. This involves their personality, values, opinions, attitudes, interests, and lifestyles. Knowing their psychographics gives you an understanding of their thought processes and reasoning behind those feedbacks. Out of the abundance of the heart comes action. People rarely say or do what they have not thought about. How and why people act is largely based on:

- where they are in their lives
- what their behaviors and attitudes are
- what they value and care about
- where they focus their energy

The questions that are not answered despite having knowledge of your consumers' demographics are often answered by insight into their psychographics. When you do not know the demographics of your audience, use their psychographics to your advantage. Let us consider the example of the previously mentioned Ghanaian chef with a different twist. Let us assume that the chef did not know the race or geographical location of the commentator. The "quality" of his/her comment will give away so much that will inform the chef whether or not his/her comment is worth considering or not. If you are an upcoming poet and you get critiqued on a poem you posted on Facebook from both a seasoned poet and a novice, which of them will it be prudent to consider? That of the seasoned poet obviously. Where people are in their lives reflects so much in the words they use and the way they act.

It is easier to react to feedbacks when you already know the background of your audience, but this is not always the situation, especially on social media where more people tend to live fake lives than real lives. People only show the glam in their lives. You may not be a psychologist to know why people act, especially those who you are not privy to their backgrounds, but you could take cues from the choice and "kind" of words they use. For example, people who are hurt in life tend to use hurtful words on others; those with low self-esteem tend to be condescending; bullies are known to have suffered bullying earlier in life, etc. When such people comment on your posts or give you feedback, take them with a pinch of salt.

The choice of words of people reflects their values, their attitudes, as well as their behaviors. For instance, if you are an advocate for feminine empowerment and you get a misogynistic comment under one of your social media posts, there is no need to go down the road of argument with such a person because both of your values are parallel and will never intersect. People do not develop values overnight, so do not expect to change someone's perspectives and values with an argument or a few hours of conversation. You may even end up losing the support you may have garnered from others on your social media platform by a wrong choice of word, which may slip out doing your rebuttal.

Don't just take people's negative response to your sample as "it is because they hate me." Even with your sworn enemies, when you take time to analyze their psychographics, the reasons for their "hostility" will not surprise you anymore. Hate is energy, though negative. Do not spend it even on your enemy because you will need all the energy you can amass when you are building a brand!

You do not need an extensive investigation into the demographics or psychographics of people who received your sample, because even minimum knowledge and acknowledgment of these is sufficient to understand the reasons behind their feedbacks. A perceived "stern" comment from an expert in your chosen field could actually be the redirection you need to better your brand. On the other hand, a perceived "reinforcing" feedback from a "fan" might actually be detrimental to your brand, hence a need to be knowledgeable of the background of your audience. Knowledge indeed is power, as you could convert even the negative energies some commentators throw at you into positive energy to help you to "better your brand."

FIVE

BETTER YOUR BRAND

> The oak fought the wind and was broken, the
> willow bent when it must and survived.
>
> —Robert Jordan

The word "better" is used here as a verb, not as a "comparative." This is because the ultimate goal we want to achieve is not a "better" brand but "the best brand." This step of *sell a brand* is the junction of the whole process. Depending on the path you take, you either walk on to your glory or your gloom. This step can be likened to the assembly department of an automobile company. When your product leaves "the assembly department," you have little control over it once it is released out to the public. Any adjustments you have to make has to be done at this stage. Remember, the best of you is what must be out there. After you have gathered and analyzed the results of your feedback in the context of the demographics and psychographics of your consumers, the next step is to make adjustments.

It is said that only a fool does not change his mind. Your product may be adjusted to meet the needs of your consumers, but your core values should not change. Several car manufacturers make cars of the same model with some differences suited to the part of the globe the car is going to be used in. A simple example is a Mercedes Benz meant to be driven in New York will have its steering wheel to the left of the car while the same model meant to be driven in London will have it to the right. You are improving on your product and personalizing it, not changing the product entirely.

You should be careful not to shift focus. When you lose focus on the originality of your brand and start compromising, you defeat the purpose of your brand. Bettering your brand can be tricky. Most people confuse it with "rebranding." Rebranding is a whole different topic. You can only rebrand when you are already a brand. At this point in the journey, you are a brand-in-the-making, but not yet a brand. If you do due diligence with your brand, it will be rare for you to have the need to rebrand. As an entrepreneur, you should aim at avoiding rebranding. Imagine the company Apple coming out to say they are rebranding. That means changing the logo, image, and a whole lot! The last chapter of this book will talk more about brand sustenance.

After your feedback, you know exactly which direction you should be taking your product. You have a fair idea of how the world will receive your product as well as what to give, who to give to, and when to give. Although you have not sold out your product yet, you know the things to add or take out to meet the needs of your consumers.

Put in your best resources because this is the final production hub of your product. Gather from everywhere necessary to get the best product. You may be familiar with the biblical account of Noah's ark. Noah was required to gather pairs of every kind of animal and keep them safe in the ark so that they could procreate following the deluge in order to prevent the various species from going extinct.

Myth or not, do you think Noah just looked around his environs and just took whichever animal he could find? I doubt that. I believe he had to actively search for some of them. If you require getting resources that are not available in your locality to build your brand, acquire them. Travel to obtain needed tools and materials if you have to. Remember that you are building a brand for posterity. Arthur Guinness in 1759 did not brew beer to last for just a decade; he thought of a brand that will linger even after he was no more. If you are a budding musician and you have great songs that you want to bring out, hire professionals with great studios and equipment. Do not settle for less. Compose timeless music, not just music to satisfy the current frenzy. When we mention pop music, one name cannot be left out. You and I know who, so I need not even mention the name. The amount of hard work and dedication put into the music makes this person's music timeless.

When you better your talent, that is when you get to be called "skilled." When only one person has to be chosen among a host, the skillful gets chosen ahead of the talented. All the highly celebrated people in this world, no matter what field, are not just talented but skilled within their respective fields.

Meager building blocks do not build mega houses. Make quality investment in your product. Cheap unprofessional workforce and materials are much more costly in the long term. Work with people who are smarter than you (not to be confused with those who will outsmart you) if you want to go far; there is so much you could learn from them to improve on yourself. When you collaborate with geniuses, it stimulates you to improve on yourself.

Your preparation tool usually reflects your degree of preparedness. Imagine wanting to learn how to play as a professional concert pianist. No matter the passion and talent you may have, if you practice with a two-octave $5 toy piano, you would not be prepared enough to play as proficiently as the masters play. In hunting a bigger animal, a smaller animal is often sacrificed as bait; however, you can't use a grasshopper as a setup to capture a lion. Therefore, employ the best resources for your brand because the money, time, talent, and other forms of investments you make today toward your brand will pay off in the long term.

Originals do not fear competition. Once your product is out there, others will attempt to replicate it. It would not be the first; neither would it be the last time for it to happen. Do well to register it and own its copyright, for obvious reasons. If you did a good work according to chapter 1 and put in quality time and resources into finishing your product, no competition should give you sleepless nights. Consumers may have preferences, but anyone who wants to have quality services, such as yours, will not compromise getting yours. When bettering your brand, your aim should not be to exceed expectations of your competitors but to excel in your originality and ingenuity. Your own dream should be your biggest competitor. Improve upon your brand until it is so solid that it can stand the test of time and counterfeits. Do not be jealous of people who offer similar services as you. The movie *Avengers Endgame* garnered so much viewers in the first week of its premiering regardless of there being other equally good movies premiering that week. Your product should be so good that when you are out of stock, you shouldn't fear to refer a customer to the nearest person who offers similar services, because you are confident they would return when you restock. There a lot of malt drinks, but no other malt drink tastes the same as Malta Guinness, and consumers know that!

At this crossroads of the journey to a successful brand, if you are confused as to which direction you are headed, go back to the basics:

your values. Your values should always keep you in check. They should be your go-to algorithm when you are stuck or perplexed. Your competitors may have some features that may seem to be beneficial if added to your product but may not be in line with your values. There is nothing wrong in borrowing ideas from others, but be wary of ideas that contradict your values. Do not compromise. The only way you can be counted in the midst of the lot is for you to stand out. Do not copy blindly. If you need to learn from a competitor to better your own brand, by all means do. Your focus should be on your brand though. No two athletes in a sprint race run in the same lane. Most people get the answers to life's questions wrong because they are usually busy reading the questions from other people's scripts/ lives. The temptation to copy a seemingly successful person is very high, but you must be confident in your own process. So far as you are on the right track, you will definitely arrive at your destination if you keep on moving forward.

Take calculated risks. Everything worthy of having is worth risking for. I am not saying part with all your savings or resources, but trust your intuition. There is a "spirit" in every human. It speaks to us every day. It is that small voice inside your head that told you to go ahead and propose to that amazing woman who has been your sweet wife for all these amazing years. It is that same voice that urged you to choose that successful career of yours when all your friends and family had alternate ideas. Sometimes your intuition may just be "common sense." As a matter of fact, with the exception of common sense, all our senses are labile. This is the secret of magicians and tricksters. They manipulate people's senses for them to believe their acts. Be guided by your values, results of your feedback, and your instincts/intuitions when bettering your brand. This is the best of you that you are going to be putting out there.

When bettering your product, do not only aim at satisfying the functional needs of consumers, but their emotional needs as well. Have you wondered why Apple users buy any product the company brings out regardless of how expensive they may be? It is because of the emotional attachment they have to the brand. A functional need is the primary purpose for which a consumer uses a service or buys a product, while an emotional need or psychological need is the sentiments one attaches to the product. With the exception of a few products, most products have already been discovered, hence you may not be the only one offering this "range" of products even though yours may be unique. That being said, people may have many options when looking for a product to satisfy their functional needs. However, what will cause a person to keep coming back every time and even recommend your products to others is the emotional connection they have with your product.

Imagine being a warm cold-water vendor in a park, with small umbrellas and chairs for patrons to relax for some few minutes while they drink their water. The water they buy satisfies their functional need of thirst while your warmness and the comfort under the shade satisfy their emotional needs. Always look for ways to satisfy your consumers' emotional needs. Satisfaction of consumer's emotional needs comes in many forms. It starts from your first contact with them to the last impression you leave on them. A simple warm greeting as a consumer enters your shop, to offering a sincere apology when all their needs are not met may be all the emotional satisfaction a consumer may be looking for. Always look for innovative ways to satisfy your consumers' emotional needs. The phrase "The customer is always right" was coined to serve this purpose.

Your brand goes beyond the traditions of your locality. Unless you plan to be a "local champion," you must think globally. Do not use local "easygoing" etiquettes when dealing with consumers, especially for those you will be dealing with online. You might not know their socialization. Always be professional. Professionalism is a universal language; every consumer understands it. Being informal or semiformal with consumers creates a bond between you and them and may make them feel at ease in dealing with you. However, cultures are different so to avoid misinterpretation of your "friendliness" by consumers, especially those you may not know personally, be as respectfully formal as much as possible.

I once had an encounter with a budding entrepreneur who happened to be in a different time zone from me. I wanted to purchase an item from her online, so I contacted her at a time which was evening for me and dawn for her. We started the transaction only for her to cut me in the middle of the business when I needed clarifications, with the excuse that it is too late to have business conversations and so she had to retire to bed. I was stunned at her rudeness. She assumed I was in the same time zone with her when I later confronted her of how unprofessional she was. She implied that she would have acted differently had she known I was an international client. Regardless of the location of your client, you should maintain high professional etiquette whether they are locals or foreigners.

Nelson Mandela is quoted to have said, "If you talk to a man in a language he understands, that goes to his head. If you talk to him in his language, that goes to his heart." As you better your product, also learn and speak the global language of dealing with consumers: professionalism. Their minds may lead them to buy from you because you meet their functional needs, but their hearts will make them come back again and again.

When you are able to better your product, you end up with the *ultimate best brand.*

SIX

SELL IT OUT B-I-G

When you find yourself in a fistfight, hit first and hit hard. That may be the first and only blow of the fight.

Meninchie

You do not need a diploma in marketing to sell your brand. Everyone is an innate seller. For the job position you currently occupy, you had to sell your worth and expertise to your current employer before you were hired. If you are a student, you had to prove your intelligence by passing a standardized test or application review before getting admitted to your school. Likewise, your brand will not get out to the world until you sell it out.

After you have done a good work on yourself, your sample becomes good, and after bettering it, it becomes the best. It then merits being sold. When people have a feel of your sample, they look forward to experiencing the "finished" product. The fallow period spent bettering your brand incites consumer hunger. After having a feel of the "good" sample you gave out, your consumers will be anticipating the finished product. Very good rappers are aware of this tactic. That is why usually before they release an album, they come up with "freestyle raps" or "singles." This whets the appetite of their audience or listeners and makes them look out for more songs from them.

All the brands you have heard of had to be put out there. You may have to register your brand to have copyrights over your products. At this stage, you are a full brand and hence you must have self-worth. Never look down on yourself. No matter how unappealing your physical nature may seem, your brand can sell. The world-famous classical music composer Ludwig van Beethoven was deaf when he wrote some of his greatest masterpieces, and the list of renowned classical musicians cannot be complete without his name. Franklin D. Roosevelt, thirty-second president of the United States of America and one of the most influential presidents, was a paraplegic. Andrea Bocelli, the marvelous opera singer whose voice has been described as "the singing voice of God" by one of the greatest vocalists, Celine Dion, is blind.

What really is your excuse for shelving your brand? There are a whole lot of people with lesser qualifications than you, working at places you are even overqualified for, living your dream life. The difference is, they chose to believe in their worth and did not just sit down but took action by selling out their relevance. An alarm can only wake you up, but you have to do the getting up yourself. Likewise, you must make a conscious effort to sell your brand.

Without a seller, there cannot be a buyer. As a human, you have needs and wants. To fulfill those needs and wants, you need to provide value in exchange. The universe gives only when it is given to. Disabuse your mind of entitlement attitude. Once you sell out your worth to the right consumer, you will be paid your due. You may have the most brilliant idea and might have even gone ahead to develop it, but if you do not get it out there, it would forever remain an idea. All the great teachers—Jesus Christ, Muhammad, Aristotle, Socrates, and others—would not have been known if they had not left their homes and taught others their beliefs. Some of them had to go up mountains, climb onto boats, talk to people that traditionally they should have avoided, and travelled from city to city in order to get their messages abroad. I cannot overemphasize it enough that you must embody your brand. You must eat it, dress it, walk it, talk it, live it! This increases consumers' confidence in your brand. If it is a product, you must always have some on you because you never know when you might meet a buyer. Have your business card handy.

People have the erroneous impression that money is evil. Money has never been evil. Many people have been indoctrinated to believe that the rich are evil. They grow up hating the rich, but the irony is that they end up working for them to fend for themselves and their families. Do not hate the player; learn the rules of the game! In fact, if money was not invented, the world would have been uninhabitable. It would have been more than a jungle here, full of chaos and disorder. Money was invented to maintain the orderly exchange of goods and services.

Many people confuse wealth with money. Wealth is the abundance of valuable possession or resource while money is a system or medium used to acquire a good or service that is desired. You cannot buy milk with wealth; you buy it with money. Acquisition of one's wants and needs brings about satisfaction and happiness; that is why everyone is striving to make enough money. You may have so much wealth in the form of intelligence, beauty, industriousness, etc., but until you are able to convert these into money, you will not be able to acquire your wants and desires. Africa is one of the wealthiest continents because it possesses vast resources—human capacity, mineral elements, favorable weather, etc.—yet it is one of the "poorest" continents because it is not able to meet most of its wants and needs. It behooves on its people to recognize the treasure they "sit" on and use it appropriately to their collective advantage. Africans are the solution to African's problems.

There is widespread misinterpretation of the dogma "The love of money is the root of evil." It is a simple phrase that requires deep wisdom to understand. Money per se is not "the evil," it is "the love of it" that is evil. Loving money means chasing it, being obsessed with it, going at all length regardless of values, giving one's life away to acquire it. This is what has led many into unwanted situations. Those who acquire it rightly do not do the above. If you chase money, you will never catch it. Make money; do not chase after it. For the simple in understanding, the root of evil in our world today is "the lack of money." Even for the wealthy families who rose to prominence via criminal activities, the heads of those houses are not the ones who wield the weapons to carry out the heinous activities. They are too rich for that! It is the one who lacks money who does that. In countries where politicians rig elections, you never see the children or the politicians themselves going to carry away ballot boxes. They are too rich for that. It is the pauper whom they hire to do their dirty work. So now, ask yourself, is it money or the lack of it which causes evil? Guns do not kill people; people do!

You need to make money because it is the current medium of exchange of value in our world. The lack and want of money have led people to do terrible things. It is all right to want money, but you need to acquire it rightly, that is why you must be a brand. Because your brand is your moneymaker. If you sell it well, you will live a fulfilled and affluent life with less stress. When you work and live your passion early in life, it feels like you never worked a day in your life. You have to trade what you have (your wealth) to get what you want, but you have to go *big* or go home! Sell it out *big*. Do not undersell your worth. Marcus Licinius Crassus, the Roman general and politician, retorted, "Greed is a word the jealous inflict on the ambitious." There is no such thing as having too much money. There is always room to make more.

Every achiever dreamt big. As you strive for excellence, you will naturally attract haters and naysayers. Do not be perturbed. I have observed that athletes are some of the most boastful professionals ever. They buy very expensive cars, houses, yachts, private jets, accessories, and other luxurious properties, and they make sure everyone knows about them. Some do it to draw attention for people to follow and purchase their products or services; others do it for self-gratification; and others for reasons best known to them. I am always happy for them when I see them enjoying the fruits of their labor. So far as they acquired them genuinely and do not denigrate others in the process, people should wish them well in their success. The worker indeed deserves his/her wages! The amount of sweat, at times even blood, they put into their training is worth every enjoyment they do after their victories.

Similarly, some people often complain that physicians and surgeons charge so much for just a few minutes of a procedure they do. Truth is, they are not charging for the procedure; they are charging for the effort, money, time, energy, and other resources they committed into their training to be able to do such procedures in no time. When you consider this, you will realize the fee being paid is just an infinitesimal amount of his or her skill. Some of the shortest plants have the deepest roots, indeed! The time spent in preparing for any great thing is usually longer than the delivery itself. For this reason, when it comes to delivering or selling out your relevance, you cannot afford to sell yourself short. People do not really care about the effort you put into your preparation; they care about the value you are selling to them. Let people know your worth. This is not mere boasting, but let them know that you are second to none in your niche. Great boxers are very good at selling themselves out *big* when they are promoting their fights. The same with great rappers. They know they put in their all and there is no way anyone else will know that or even imagine their struggle. So they put their struggles into words and trumpet it out to people.

There are several selling strategies. In today's technological world, selling has become even way easier. All the strategies described under the chapter "Give a Free Sample," can be employed in selling your brand out. The only difference is that this time, you are going out *big*! If you require more people to help to get your brand out there, do so. This may involve hiring marketers to put your products out there, going on radio and TV shows, embarking on tours, posting on social media, organizing concerts, shows, workshops, getting stands at events to showcase your wares and digital marketing. At this stage, you have to be nosy for opportunities and noisy to be heard. Be attentive, alert, aggressive, and ever ready to sell out to a buyer.

Timidity is often confused with humility. The latter is good for your brand, but the former kills dreams and opportunities. No one is born timid, so do not make excuses with that attribute. Timidity is an acquired behavior of lack of courage and confidence. People who are timid are easily frightened. Success and fear are not compatible. You must curb fear and shyness in order to get your product out there. Sometimes your patrons are people you least expect, hence be ready in season and out of season with your product. You never know who might be interested.

Selling out your brand *big* does not mean selling at an exorbitant price. Several factors go into the determination of a price on a brand. Not all costly items are great and not all affordable products are substandard. Your price depends on the value of your brand to the buyer. Value does not have a price tag. Those who know what they need, and are able to recognize it, will part with whatever they have, to acquire their need. If you are able to get your consumer to fully recognize why they need your brand, you do not have to worry about what price to quote to them; the job of selling is more than 70 percent done. The value of your product to your buyer determines to a large extent how much they would be willing to pay. You will be paid your due when you sell to the right consumer.

A story is told of a father who bequeathed an antique wristwatch to his son. He told the son the watch's worth and asked him to take the watch to a jewelry shop to find out how much they will be willing to pay for the watch. The son returned and told the father that the jeweler offered to pay about a tenth of the watch's worth because they said the watch was so old. He again sent him to a pawnshop to find out how much they would offer for the watch. The son again returned to his father and told him they offered to pay him a hundredth of the watch's worth because they said it was so worn out. He sent him out one more time to a museum to inquire how much they would offer for the watch. He returned to his father and told him that the curator offered twice the worth of the watch saying that it was a rare piece and the museum would wish it were part of their collection. You need to know your worth and sell to those who recognize it too.

Before you put a price on your product, be sure and confident about it. You don't want to quote one price today and quote a different one the following day. Consumers appreciate decisive brands. The prices of similar brands may give you a range of how much to charge, but do not depend solely on them. Always do a value check.

Remember to be respectful and humble when dealing with consumers. Some people will misconstrue your confidence as arrogance, but do not let that deter you from promoting your brand.

Musicians do not go on music tours just for the fun of traveling but because even great music without wide publicity will not sell. Even a mediocre musician with a great promotion team can outsell a super talented and prolific musician who does less promotion of their musical works. The reason why you might hear great musical pieces by a certain musician, however the musician is still not widely known is because of poor promotion. A living dog is indeed better than a dead lion.

You need to promote your brand by selling it out *big*. Unless it is solely for pro bono purposes, every selling venture should have a serious business management team. If you cannot manage the business aspect yourself, acknowledge it and solicit a trusted business manager with favorable terms. You may engage the services of a family member like what most brands started with or traditional businessmen/women, but you need to lay down formal terms of engagement. Remember, it is a business, so do not let other emotions and sentiments get in the way. A good business management team is one of the biggest elements some brands lacked and died poor. One of the greatest classical music composers whose music sends chills down the spine till date, Wolfgang Amadeus Mozart, died at a young age of thirty-five and was buried in a "common grave" despite his musical ingenuity largely because of poor business management.

There are several notable famous people who did not pay much attention to the business aspects of their brands and suffered poverty for it. In as much as it is important to give your audience a great show if you a performer, you should also pay heed to the business aspect as well because when the curtains are lowered and the lights are dimmed, you face your "demons" alone. Pay attention to the "biz" part of *showbiz!* Do the *show* for the masses, but do not forget to do the *biz* for you. You are a big shot, so sell yourself out *big*.

SEVEN

Maintain your brand

You rest, you rust.

As you may have noticed, all the steps in *Sell a Brand* are action statements. The last step is no exception. This is because being a successful brand is not just a state of being; it is a continuous process of activities. You are not successful yet until you can maintain your brand. See this step as the "roofing of the house." The roofing of a house is equally important as the foundation. When the classical elements—earth, water, air, fire, and ether—strike against a building, its survival rests on the tenacities of the foundation and the roofing.

Maintenance involves actions performed to keep a system functioning or in service. Your brand needs to continue functioning. Your brand must live long enough for you to benefit from it. You may not be alive to see its full potential, but you should be able to see it thrive. The beauty of brands is that it gives immortality to a person. A person may be dead and gone, but the brand may still live on. All personal and product brands that are sought after today are being maintained by somebody somewhere. There has to be active management of your brand if you want to stay relevant. The effort you put in maintaining it may not be the same as you did at the starting point though. The fact that most billionaires and entrepreneurs make wealth even while they "sleep" does not mean their businesses are also "sleeping."

A sleeping business is a dead business! The owners may be sleeping, but someone somewhere is laboring in their stead. There is literally no rest in the journey of success. You may be physically resting, but work has to be put into your brand at every time for your brand to remain significant. Your brand has to always be in motion. If you abandon a house for a long time and do not maintain it, it begins to harbor uninvited guests and may even eventually end up collapsing. If you wish to see your brand survive, you must continuously put in work.

Maintaining a brand can be akin to driving an automobile. There are times you put your foot on the gas pedal and at other times you put them on the brakes. If you are driving a manual transmission, you will need to change gears occasionally. Even with your foot off all pedals, you still use your hands to steer the wheel. There is never a time you go to bed while you are driving, even for automatic transmission vehicles. There is nothing like absolute autopilot when you own a brand. Building a brand is not for the faint of heart. The following are measures to guide you as you maintain your brand.

1. **Consistency**

    The fuel of every brand is in consumer confidence and patronage. Building personal relationships with consumers is helpful, but that is not enough to keep them "loyal" to your brand. Once your patrons realize you no longer uphold the core values with which they have associated your brand, they will begin to look elsewhere for that satisfaction they once had from you. People appreciate honest and truthful businesses. Give your patrons their investment's or money's worth. No matter what, give them what they pay for. They may finish using your product or services, but they will always remember the value for their money, time, and energy you gave them. Never ruin your integrity by cutting corners and giving out substandard performances. If your brand is a true reflection of yourself, you would not have to struggle to be consistent. You just have to keep on doing and being you.

If you have come this far to build a brand, you should not let other brands distract you. You may take constructive critiques to manage your brand, but your core values and goal should under no circumstance be altered. Be sure to differentiate critiques from criticisms. The former is based on detailed analysis and assessment of your performance while the latter is mostly based on perceived faults or mistakes to show sheer disapproval. Critiques are meant to improve you, but criticisms usually come from naysayers and are often intended to discourage and disparage you, so be discerning. Stay clear of such people.

I respect every brand for one reason: their consistency. It does not matter the field, belief system, personality, etc., of the person. If a brand is not consistent, you would not even get to hear about it for long enough because anything that is not consistent dies a "natural" death, usually prematurely. Nature has a way of bringing out the best in people. It does by pushing people around until they have been duly refined to be their best version.

Consistency is closely related to hard work, but the two are very different. Hard work can make you successful, but consistency makes you a master. With consistency, you are more dependable and trustworthy because you routinely achieve the same level of success and complete tasks no matter how long they take. The consistency of all the brands you know of today is what has kept them relevant till date while their contemporaries languished. The contemporaries of all the successful people you can think of today are no longer their current competitors. It is their consistency that sets them apart and has brought them this far. You really should be asking yourself some serious questions if your competitors at the time you start up a business or enterprise are still the only people competing with you at the peak of your business. You should be miles ahead of them!

It is said that consistency is harder when no one is clapping for you. You surely have to clap for yourself during those times because you should always be your biggest fan. Sometimes, the cheers from friends, family, and loved ones to keep you going may fade. Still, keep the wheels turning. Familiarity breeds contempt. Sometimes, people may become too "familiar" with you and your brand that they may seem to take you for granted. Stand firm and uphold your brand regardless. Do not kowtow to seemingly new trends at the detriment of your originality. This is not to say be stiff-necked. Be dynamic with your originality. This is the key to survival of every brand.

Being dynamic means adapting. It is said that the dinosaurs

could not adapt to their environment, that is why they are extinct. Truth or just fable, a lesson can be learned from it. With time, younger and more vibrant brands will begin to rival yours, but bear in mind that the taste of satisfaction of humans does not know age! Once your product is still relevant to your consumers, the longer you have been in existence becomes a validation for you instead of an obsolescence. This is because consistency brings with it a reputation of being reliable and trustworthy. Be dynamically consistent!

2. **Hard work**

Hard work is often confused with tough work. A lot of people use them interchangeably. Hard work means getting the work done no matter what it takes. Tough work means labor. The poor construction site worker does not work any harder than the affluent entrepreneur in the luxurious air-conditioned office. There are no guarantees with tough work, but there surely is success at the end of hard work. If it takes tough work to get the work done, so be it. If it takes working smarter to get the work done, so be it. That is hard work! Most people are scared of inquiring about the secret of success because they fear they would be told that it is *hard work.*

Unfortunately, there is no substitute for hard work. You have to stay on the grind. There is no shortcut for it. It is what it is. Hard work is the secret recipe the rich and great have that the poor and meager lack. The great sculptor, painter, architect, and poet Michelango di Lodovico Buonarroti Simoni retorted, "If people knew how hard I had to work to gain my mastery, it would not seem so wonderful at all." After you have built your brand, you have to continue working hard to maintain it. Do not rest on your oars. Keep on putting in effort into your brand.

Staying at the top is more difficult than being at the bottom. It is not greed that causes the wealthy to stay up late at night in the first-class cabin of an airplane while the middle-class snore in the economy cabin. It is the desire and determination to remain at the top. Many people erroneously assume the rich book first-class cabins out of extravagance. Majority of them actually do so to have privacy to work while they travel. The next time you book a long trip air flight, take a peek at the first-class cabin while the lights are off in the economy cabin with people sleeping and you would be amazed at the number of active laptop screens with their owners busily working. This is not to say to never rest when you get to the top but keep up the energy. Be consistently hardworking!

3. **Remember your beginnings**

Life is lived forward but understood backward. Most if not all successful brands had humble beginnings. Remember two key things about your beginnings: what you stand for and how far you have come. I would not want to belabor the point about holding on to your core values. The focus of this bulletin is going to be on the latter. Sometimes, it is not the strength in a man that causes him to outrun others but the force after him. If you do not see anything good that has happened to you for you to celebrate, think of the worst things you have escaped. Many people died with their visions unrealized, but you still draw breath and have potential.

Your brand may not as yet be where you envisioned it to be, but a grateful heart is all sometimes you need as motivation. There are times you might feel like giving up. In such times, look back, see how far you have come, dust yourself up, celebrate your little victories, and stride on. Gratitude goes beyond religion; it is a self-upliftment virtue you must learn to maintain your brand. Show genuine appreciation to your consumers because your brand is irrelevant if it isn't serving anyone. You can only show genuine appreciation if you have a grateful heart. Always be grateful.

I once entered a new convenience shop that had recently opened near our house to say hello to the owner to establish acquaintance as our new neighbors. There were two gentlemen at the counter. Both greeted me warmly when I entered and bid me farewell when I exited. I observed that one's farewell as I exited was out of duty while the other did so with a tone of appreciation. Without asking anyone, I could tell who the owner of the store was from the caretaker. The owner showed appreciation to attract buyers and retain customers while the caretaker was nonchalant. Appreciation, like love, is a universal language; it doesn't require an interpreter. When you are grateful for how far your brand has come, you would put in your best to keep it running.

See life and everything that you have achieved as a privilege, not as a right. Most people are bitter in life because they have an entitlement attitude. Save yourself the heartache. There are times in life when the inevitable happens. For example: losses, failures, disappointments, trials, betrayals, humiliations, natural disasters, pandemics, etc. The COVID-19 pandemic, which caused alteration of everyone's life one way or the other, is a typical example of the limitations of humans and the gratification of all our desires in the face of unforeseen eventualities.

Despite putting in your best effort, sometimes things may not turn out the way you envisioned. In such times, you need the serenity to accept that you cannot control everything. The world does not revolve around you alone; you are a part of a bigger purpose than yourself. When you live devoid of the "entitlement attitude," you are able to handle life's misfortunes better.

Acknowledge that you have limitations. There is only so much you have control over. Remember your humble beginnings and be grateful for how far you have come and how much misfortune you have escaped.

4. **Continuous learning**

One of the exercises which you continue to do from the time you are born till you die is learning. You learned how to crawl, walk, talk, read, write, drive, fly a plane, sing, sew, operate on people, etc. Everything changes and so should your knowledge. What you do not know, you cannot do. To keep your brand in existence, you need to constantly update your information. The information you had yesterday, as of today, is outdated. Be abreast of time. The most powerful people in the world today are the ones who have information and use them. It comes as no surprise that the world's most powerful countries invest so much in acquiring pertinent information both home and abroad because they know their immense value. This is termed "intelligence." When the human race finished exploring every corner of the earth, they then ventured into space, not for a fun trip, but to acquire more "intelligence."

It isn't just enough to acquire the knowledge; you need to utilize it. Continue to invest in relevant information acquisition. Look out for and attend seminars, classes, symposiums, lectures, workshops, talks related to your brand. Read books, journals, articles about ideas, especially those related to your brand. Engage level-headed people in discussing ideas. It is said that small brains discuss people, medium brains discuss events, but big brains discuss ideas.

Be fond of discussing ideas, even if it means discussing it with yourself. Because most of the time, that is when you have "eureka" moments. You need to be up to date with current trends even if you are not the one directly running your company or business. Do not just hire people and close your mind to self-development. No useful knowledge is antagonistic to the human brain. I like to refer to the brain as a "muscle" because like regular muscles, the more you exercise it, the tougher and stronger it becomes. The brain is very precious, so it comes as no surprise that it is covered by one of the strongest bones, the calvarium. Ask questions and you will find answers because anyone who seeks, gains. This is the secret of ingenuity.

After you have learned more in your niche, be curious about your environment and continuously increase your knowledge about it. As I stated in earlier chapters, all brands are interconnected one way or the other, so you need to know about others as well. We now live in a smaller world because of technology. It does not take so much to find information about your environment. This does not mean go about poking your nose into other people's businesses but have a fair idea of what is going on around you. This may even help you to find opportunities and avenues around you that you can take advantage of.

It is also important for security reasons. Knowledge about your community helps you to know where to expand your businesses, which areas to avoid, and which people to deal or not deal with. Know your business inside out and mind it. There should be nothing about your brand that you should not be able to answer questions on. Be a guru of your brand. This can only be achieved when you *mind your own business!*

5. **Partnership**

There is a popular Akan adage that translates as "One man's hands cannot cover the eye of God." Another African proverb states, "If you want to go fast, go alone; if you want to go far, go together." You cannot do it all, all the time. You may have started your business or company alone, but along the path, you may need to partner with others. This does not make you less of a brand. Recognizing the need to partner with others is the zenith of business maturity.

Partnership, especially business partnership, is a legal form of business operation between two or more entities who share management, losses, and profits. It could be a verbal agreement or documented. No matter how informal it may be, for example, if it is with your wife, husband, child, brother, mother, father or cousin, business partnerships are legal and should be treated as such. When your brand becomes a business, you need to partner with others if you wish to make profits. Bear in mind that making profit off your brand is not evil.

There are several varieties of partnership, but the basic ones are general and limited partnerships. In the former, partners manage the company and assume responsibility for the partnership's debts and other obligations while the latter serve as investors. The investment could be in terms of their money, time, services, other resources. Limited partners have no control over the company and are not subject to the same liabilities as general partners. Partnership in simple terms means working with others to handle some of the affairs of your brand.

See everyone who works with or for you as a partner. Those not involved in executive functions are the limited partners, for example, employees; while general partners include mergers, acquisitions, shareholders, etc. Acknowledge your workers as "team members" rather than just "employees" because the former gives them a greater sense of belonging. They may not take executive actions in the company, but it makes them feel that their inputs are valuable to your brand. This in itself is motivation for them as they work with you. Even though limited partners are labile, because they could just get up one day and leave your business, both general and limited partners should be appreciated and treated with respect. Team members tend to work wholeheartedly to support your vision as a brand when you treat them with dignity and consider their welfare. Take great care of your team members and they will take great care of your clients! As a brand you will need to work with partners, general and limited.

The bigger your brand becomes, the more hands you may require to fill various portfolios. The day you became a brand is the day you became the CEO. You command the power to hire and fire and you should not be afraid to do either or both when the situation demands.

There may be several qualities you may be looking for in your partners, such as hard work, punctuality, knowledge, etc., but the most important one should be people who share and understand your goals and core values. Never compromise on this. No matter how well sought after a partner is or how promising they appear, if they are not convinced of your goals or core values, they are not worth partnering with. Unless two people agree, they cannot walk together! The document of acceptance of a partnership signed on paper is irrelevant if the body, soul, and mind of your partner are not into what you as a brand stands for. The kind of people you hire depends on the products of your brand. You may hire Miss A over Mr B for one reason or another; Miss A may have certain attributes that may be more helpful to your brand. That is fine. You cannot partner with everybody. Sometimes cutting some people loose is very difficult, but that may be the only way to go.

You need to be bold, courageous, and assertive as a brand. Be fair and firm. You do not necessarily have to hire your friends. In fact, friendship is not a criterion for hiring. Neither is family relations. The only people who should be working with you are those who bring value to your brand. Do not do people favors by giving them employment in your company if they do not make the cut. Find other avenues to help them. Iron sharpens iron. This is the core of every partnership.

The automatic arrangement of every small budding company is like a dry-cell series circuit: the dry cells represent your team members and lighted bulb represents successful end results. The bulb at the end of the circuit only lights when current flows uninterrupted through all the dry cells. A nonfunctioning dry cell will stop the current flow and prevent the bulb from lighting up. As your company grows and becomes bigger and more departmentalized, the circuit becomes a parallel one. This is dangerous for you the CEO and general partners, but quite convenient for lackadaisical limited partners (team members).This is because detecting culprits who may be dragging your brand behind may be difficult. After all, despite their inadequacies, "some" work will still be done because of the efforts of others. Overall performance may, however, be low.

Your brand is as good as your team so ensure you have the best and competent people on board. There should be checks and balances as well as the smooth running of the day-to-day activities to keep your brand on track. These functions are overseen by a board of directors/management, which is made up of you and your general partners. This makes having a working board of directors/management an indispensable element of any established brand for sustenance.

Your ultimate aim should be to build a lasting brand that even posterity will marvel at. Your legacy is not necessarily the children you bring forth because they will grow up and follow their own paths in life, but it is the solid brand you build and maintain. Success is not inherited; it is hard-earned. People who inherit great estates but do not share in the vision, values, or purpose of the originator end up losing everything they inherited. It is not enough to have a brand; it should be sustainable even after you are no more. Choosing and mentoring your successor is essential to the immortality of your legacy. Whoever you choose to continue your legacy should be under your direct tutelage and if possible, sooner than later, regardless of the formal education they acquire.

You need to wake up, build your brand, and sell it out now! Never put off till tomorrow what you can do today (Thomas Jefferson, third president of United States of America).

Epilogue

After completing this book, you should be convinced that you are not here on this planet by accident or by coincidence. You have a purpose. Your purpose is embedded in you as a *brand*. You are relevant and as such you are capable of *selling a brand* to the world. Nothing less. You do not need to prove a point to anyone. There is no need to live your life to impress anyone. In fact, you may even have to disappoint some close friends and relatives when you decide to pursue your purpose. Do not let that stop you. In the long run, they will come around and will be proud of you. You are not in competition with anyone but yourself. You have the blueprint to be successful. You only have to consistently work hard on it to perfect and maintain it. You hold all the tools to make this happen.

This journey of success must begin with your acknowledgment of the genius you are. Do not pay attention to those who make you believe you will not amount to anything. Recognize your potential because you are more than *just a mass,* you are *a force at rest!* You have momentum waiting to unleash. You will continue to be at rest (just as Sir Isaac Newton's Law of Inertia states) or not see any change in your current state of misery or discontentment unless you permit a force to act on you to change course. This force can be negative or positive depending on the results it drives you to achieve.

This book was meant to exert a positive force on you to accelerate you on to your course of success. You alone hold that power. Yes, you are that powerful. Do not give power unnecessarily to people to control your life. You alone can give permission to anyone or anything to have an effect on you.

You were born to be a *brand*, but unless you recognize it, materialize it, sell it out, and live as such, you will merely fade into memory. Everything you dream about or envision can be brought into existence. Mobilize the right tools that this book has revealed and you will be on your way there. And while you are at it, do not stain *the brand!*

Do not forget that the world is full of people at different stages in their lives. Do not compare your nadir to the acme of someone's life, no matter the age of the person. Everything is a process. You have to unleash that potential in you before your potential energy can be converted into kinetic energy. The universe will take whatever you give it, so do not coil in your shell. The universe awaits you.